Stop Right There.

A Book about Periods

by Marie Powell
illustrated by Anthony Lewis

amicus readers 3

amicus readers

Say Hello to Amicus Readers.

You'll find our helpful dog, Amicus, chasing a ball—to let you know the reading level of a book.

1

Learn to Read

Frequent repetition, high frequency words, and close photo-text matches introduce familiar topics and provide support for brand new readers.

2

Read Independently

Some repetition is mixed with varied sentence structures and a select amount of new vocabulary words are introduced with text and photo support.

3

Read to Know More

Interesting facts and engaging art and photos give fluent readers fun books both for reading practice and to learn about new topics.

Amicus Readers are published by Amicus
P.O. Box 1329, Mankato, MN 56002
www.amicuspublishing.us

Illustrations by Anthony Lewis

Produced for Amicus by The Peterson Publishing Company and Red Line Editorial.

Editor Jenna Gleisner
Designer Jake Nordby

Printed in Malaysia
10 9 8 7 6 5 4 3 2 1

Library of Congress Cataloging-in-Publication Data
Powell, Marie, 1958-
  Stop right there : a book about periods / By Marie Powell ; Illustrations by Anthony Lewis.
    pages cm. -- (Punctuation station)
  "Emma and Jane play together while learning how to correctly use periods in a sentence."
  ISBN 978-1-60753-730-4 (library binding)
  ISBN 978-1-60753-834-9 (ebook)
  1. English language--Punctuation--Juvenile literature. 2. English language--Sentences--Juvenile literature. I. Title. II. Title: Book about periods.
  PE1450.P66 2015
  428.1'3--dc23
                              2014045808

Punctuation marks help us understand writing. A period is placed at the end of a sentence to show where a sentence stops.

Emma says to her friend Jane, "Let's go play at my house today."

Emma lives across the street from school. A crossing guard tells the girls, "Stop right there."

5

6

At Emma's house, Emma's mom writes on the whiteboard.

"Mrs. Jones," says Jane. "You forgot something."

Mrs. Jones says, "No, we only need milk and bread. What did I forget?"

Jane puts two periods on the whiteboard.

She says, "A period stops sentences from running into each other."

"A period can abbreviate, or shorten, a title, too," says Jane. "I've shortened doctor to Dr."

Emma has a 10:00 appointment with

Dr. Levi

"Can we go with you to the store, Mom?" asks Emma. "I have two dollars. I could buy a snack for Jane and me."

"I baked cookies this afternoon," says Emma's mom. "You can both have one after dinner."

Emma and Jane see the plate of chocolate chip cookies.

Emma's mother says, "Stop right there. Those are for dessert."

Emma says, "This time the period stopped us."

Remember to use a period:

To end a sentence:

Stop right there.

To abbreviate, or shorten, a person's title:

Emma has a 10:00 appointment with Dr. Levi.